WEST BROADWAY

West Broadway

GEORGE STANLEY

VANCOUVER ▲ NEW STAR BOOKS ▲ 2018

NEW STAR BOOKS LTD.
No. 107 – 3477 Commercial Street, Vancouver, BC V5N 4E8   CANADA
1574 Gulf Road, No. 1517, Point Roberts, WA 98281   USA
www.NewStarBooks.com   info@NewStarBooks.com

The publisher acknowledges the financial support of the Canada Council for
the Arts and the British Columbia Arts Council.

 Canada Council   Conseil des arts   BRITISH COLUMBIA
for the Arts   du Canada   ARTS COUNCIL
                                 An agency of the Province of British Columbia

Cataloguing information for this book is available from
Library and Archives Canada, www.collectionscanada.gc.ca.

Cover design by Robin Mitchell Cranfield
Cover image: Jack Shadbolt, *Encounter*, 1995, acrylic on
board. Gift of the Doris Shadbolt Estate, 2006. © Courtesy
Simon Fraser University Galleries, Burnaby, BC
Printed and bound in Canada by Gauvin Press
First published February 2018

WEST BROADWAY

1

'Each of us has his life-world, meant as the world for all.'
EDMUND HUSSERL

Vague abstract thoughts
tinged with dread

struggle to maintain footing on the north bank (sidewalk)

Akhmatova asked how can you look at the Neva
or step onto
one of her bridges

Vague abstract thoughts cut *like sharp wings of black angels*

This river runs both ways
There are no bridges, only crosswalks
monitored by traffic lights, automated or ped-operated ('Push
    the button!')

No one knows the feelings
Yet not for nothing are they thought to be sorrowful

Raspberry bonfires bloom in the snow (St. Petersburg, 1914)

        *

This river runs both ways.

West it flows (up its tributary Tenth Avenue)
to the 'uni' (as I've heard one Ontarienne call it).

East it goes to the 'Anti-city' (Scott's word)
& a former city planner says
downtown business interests placed obstacles in the way
of development along central Broadway, seeing it
as a potential rival. From the late '50s, it becomes
Vancouver's doctor-and-dentist-land.

Fairmont Medical Building (1959). Look at the windows.
Fourteen storeys of narrow, dark offices.

Panoramic vista — 19th floor of the 'electric razor building':
North Shore mountains & the city glittery like a magic island
from the hygienist's chair, until she tips me back.

Thoughts arrive by bus, car, cab,
on ped X-ings cross Broadway,
afoot, w/cane, walker, in wheelchair;
when traffic flows again, cross Willow,
to clinic, pharmacy, lab.

   *

Tall yellow poles skim the wires,
blue trolleybuses sail by
like Swedish yachts.

99-B's travel fast, carry
stolid swaying standing students
like troop transport.

   *

4

Round midnight a dark voice,
a repetitive chant
getting closer on the north bank (sidewalk)
rises in pitch as it nears —
words become more distinct — they are words —

'Fuck Canada! Fuck Canada! Fuck Canada!
(crossing Balaclava) Fuck this goddamn country!'

& now it seems an obbligato, muted, of several voices
(as if reproving the dark voice),
coming from the south bank, in front of Timmy's —
'Canada. Canada.'

Then from a block further west a voice starts 'O Canada,'
missing the tune.

   *

Face unlovely
mix of hair & skin
emanating fury
mouth a cave
'(swallowed word) something to eat,'
takes the proffered coin,
'Thanks.'

   *

Each one's individual sequel
conceived as 'end times'

& out of a confused argument at the pub
comes:

Write Off the Salmon Streams
Pump the Bitumen Through
Maybe China Will Burn Less Coal

*

A chit? — is that it? — or credit slip — from the old
Pulpfiction, that had closed (next to the Hollywood, that had
also closed) I kept in my wallet, thinking that someday I
might wander by the new Pulpfiction (on the south bank, next
to the wine shop) & apply it to the purchase of a book. The
chit was for $4.50.

So one day I did wander by the new Pulpfiction, went in &
quickly found a book, one I had never read, a classic, *The
Epic of Gilgamesh*. The price was $7.95. I took the book to the
counter & produced my chit — half expecting it would be
considered long outdated & therefore discredited. But no —
the clerk acknowledged it as legitimate and so reduced the
price of the book to $3.45. Plus tax, that came to $3.62. I had
a few pennies in my pocket, so as I often do, I gave her two of
these to make the change (from a five) come out even — well,
no, mainly to get rid of them.

As I was handing the two pennies over to the clerk, I noticed
that one of them bore a familiar handsome face — a profile —
it took me back to my childhood — it was King George VI. I
checked the date — 1947. I pointed this out to the clerk, who
said, 'Do you want to keep it?' A moment's thought — 'Yes.'
I put it back in my pocket & came up with another (newer)
penny to give to her.

On my way home now, I stopped off at another bookstore,
Brigid's Books, where my friend Sean was seated at the desk,

reading as always. Happily I showed him the *Gilgamesh* &
said, 'If I hadn't found this, I'd probably be browsing here.'

Next stop was Parthenon, to pick up some deli items —
Jarlsberg cheese, German salami, maybe Kalamata olives, I
can't recall. The bill came to some odd sum ending in 3 or 7,
and as I had a few pennies in my pocket, I put down two or
three of them to make it come out even — well, no, mainly to
get rid of them.

Two days later: 'Where's my 1947 penny?'

They're diverting the Euphrates to build Bilgames' (the
Sumerian name for Gilgamesh) tomb.

'They breached the Euphrates, they emptied it of water,
its pebbles gazed on the Sun God in wonder.'

Gilgamesh quote from The Epic of Gilgamesh, *translated by Andrew*
George. London: Penguin Books, 1999, pp. 205–6.

2

'Oh My God,' she cried, as the walker slipped away from her & rolled rattled toward the front of the bus. A man jumped up from his seat to catch it before it hit anything & returned it to her. Then in a high, rising voice, she, heavy, grey-haired, rising from her seat before the bus had stopped (at Bayswater), called to the driver, 'I need the ramp.' At the stop, the driver opened the door & activated the ramp (which rises vertically from its seating to the perpendicular then descends to rest on the shore (i.e., sidewalk), & she, again, ponderously pushing the walker (a black metal walker with a black wire basket for purse or other goods, but hers empty), slowly exited.

Out the window on the other side of the bus I could see the events racing by, in the air, on the street.

& I could sense, invisibly, in human minds human thoughts trying to make a gain on one another, to keep up with the events, and the price of money.

No independent variables, just the one reality, runs through their brains.

*

Median burnt on King Eddie, butts.

*

Democracy = Beauty

*

S. has a tattoo
inside her upper left arm,
a pink five-petaled flower —
plumaria. Plumaria? —
how BC to have a tattoo
of a particular flower. 'Oh no,
I got it in Brazil.
I was just drunk . . .
stumbled on it.'

*

'Can you take me to the 10?' (wait a minute, the Byrider
thought, this is a 14 westbound on Broadway, how can he take
her to the 10?) 'or maybe someone can help me across the
street.'

The Byrider said he would help her across the street
(Broadway). And so he took her arm. But he held it the wrong
way — like it was an object he held in his hand — a pork chop
or something — an existential distance between it & her —
& so they stumbled a few steps (towards Granville), him in
effect pulling up on her left arm and her off-balance moving
her right leg alternately with the cane with the curved handle
she leaned on — until somehow just by trying to right herself
she got his right arm under her left. And so they proceeded
towards the northwest corner of Broadway & Granville. She
had said she wanted to get a southbound 10. This meant
crossing Broadway.

But now, as they approached the corner, she began to falter,
she began to say, 'I can't make it, I can't cross the street, I'm

afraid, I'll fall.' He tried to reassure her, 'Come on, you've made it this far, you can get across, come on.' But she slowed down & came to a stop & said, 'I can't, I'm afraid. Can you get me a cab?'

He saw a cab approaching westbound along Broadway & he tried to nudge her closer to the curb & flag it down (with his left arm, which the driver wouldn't have seen anyway) but the cab made a right turn on Granville & took off.

Across Granville he saw the dimmed lights of another cab parked by the curb glimmering. 'But I can't keep holding you up & get the cab too,' he explained. 'Here, sit down and lean on this' (a concrete garbage receptacle). She slid down & leaned on the garbage bin gripping her cane lower down so its curved handle rose above her head. The Byrider crossed Granville to where the cab was parked, thinking, I hope this guy will do this. He opened the back door of the cab, stuck his head in, & said, 'I need a cab for that lady across the street.' And the cabbie, an older Irishman, said, 'Is that her at the corner?' 'Yes.' 'Sure,' he said. The Byrider got in the back and handed the cabbie two fives across the seat. The light was green & the cab crossed over quickly. 'It's a bus stop,' the cabbie said, 'but I don't care much about buses.' The Byrider got out & helped the woman into the cab & the cabbie said, 'Where do you want to go, ma'am?' '14th & Granville.' (14th & Granville? the Byrider thought, what?) 'Yes, there's a bench there where I can lie down.'

*

Damon saw the old guy after the old guy saw him, so he knew the reason the old guy was crossing Balaclava on a bias, rather than at the corner, was to avoid him.

The old guy was now maybe twenty meters ahead of him, walking fast toward the entrance to Hollywood Manor. Damon yelled – well not very loud, it was more like a cry — something — that sounded to the old guy like 'Hey' or 'Hi.' The old guy turned around. Damon said, 'Do you live around here?'

and the old guy walked slowly — well yes, reluctantly, back toward him. Damon moved toward the old guy, jerkily, on his crutches, dragging his limp, bent legs. 'My name is Damon, I want to get to 7th & Balaclava.' 'It's two blocks.' Damon moved another step or two, his face showing pain. 'I want to see some friends of mine. I don't know if they'll be home.'

The old guy said, 'I'm sorry, I don't have a car.'

Then Damon said, 'I don't have very much food.'

Then the old guy gave him money & I guess Damon said thanks, I don't remember. The old guy then turned away, but before they broke eye contact Damon said, 'At least it's not raining. That's my silver lining.' Then the old guy walked to the door of Hollywood Manor & let himself in & when he got upstairs to his apartment he did not look out the window to see Damon drag himself by on his way to 7th.

Then the old guy gave himself shit because he knew Damon knew he had tried to avoid him.

My Room

after Baudelaire, 'La Chambre Double'

1

Did I dream this room?
A refuge for my soul,
a cell of rainbow light,

where I can bask at sundown
in negligent regret
for the passing of desire

on a chaise longue that seems
itself to dream, in the carved
sleep of furniture, under fabrics woven
of the sun's last, long rays?

No bad art on the walls!
No painstaking realism to distract
my soul from the dream's
agreeable *clair-obscur*!

A tang of cinnamon whiskey
rides on the vaporous air
as close to sleep fleeting visions
come to be slower to fade.

2

Against cascading white curtains, ensconced on a white divan,
the Queen of my Dreams, in basic black (with pearls)
lounges before my eyes. Whence came she here?
No matter. I see her. I *recognize* her.

Her eyes whose blaze migrates across the dusk,
superior eyes that subjugate their slave,
black, glossy stars that waken awe in me,
awe, admiration, and enrapturement.

Of what supernal power am I the heir,
lapped round by waves of peace and mystery?
What life had I before this marvelous dream
whose sweet perdures, minute by minute, second by second?

But wait! There are no seconds, minutes. Time's no more!
This is eternity! The realm of eternal delight!
Then there's a knock at the door.

THEN THERE'S A KNOCK AT THE DOOR!
A knock like a sock in the jaw,
a knock like a kick in the nuts.
The door opens. Three spectres enter:

1. An auditor from Revenue Canada — he wants to measure
the floor area of the room I've deducted for business purposes;

2. The kid I bought a coffee last night at Blenz — he's back to
tell me the rest of the story of his life since he left Kelowna;

3. The editor of *Thrush* (formerly *Thrust*) magazine: 'I just
happened to be in the 'hood, can I pick up that poem — "My
Room" — you promised me? Is it finished yet?'

4

My paradise collapses.
The Queen of my Dreams, all her magic
& wonderment, vanishes.

And I remember! I remember!
This hole, this pad, this cell of tedium
is mine. This is my room.

I see the dusty, ugly, box-like furniture,
the armchair leaning on its broken leg,
the grimy window, the spotted mirror,
the stack of poems, with lines or whole half-pages
    roughly crossed out,
the daytimer with doctors' appointments
    neatly penciled in.

The fragrance of an altered world,
the sense of a perfected sensibility,
are supplanted by the reek of smoke & coffee grounds,
& all around, faint but sharp in the room,
the smell of one man alone.

In this my world, where I gag with disgust,
one object seems to smile back like a friend
(like all friends, it promises flattery, then desertion).
On the carpet, by the desk, I spy a screw
of white paper, charred at one end: a fat roach.

And oh yes, Time is back, the louche old King,
attended by his wretched retinue
of Thoughts, Memories, Shame, Remorse,
Apprehension, Premonition, Worry, Anxiety
(& let's not forget To-do Lists).

The red second hand unbudges & starts its trek
across the barren steppe to the next tick,
and as each joyous second leaps from the clock's face,
it turns cartwheels in the air & cries:
'I am Life! The life you cannot live,
the life you cannot not live.'

There is just one second in a person's life
whose role it is to bring really good news.
But why is it, *la bonne nouvelle* causes
such terror in everyone who hears it?

Time wears the big hat. Life is his rancho.
And me he drives like a panting, running steer.
The Range Boss leans from his saddle & taps me with his
    taser:
'Get along, dogie! Head down, slave! Live, loser!'

Our Age (an imitation)

after Anna Akhmatova

Why is this age worse than all those preceding?
Because deranged by greed and desirous of pleasure,
we borrowed against the cancer that was eating us,
the wound we could not close.

West Point Grey chills in late sunlight,
sun's rays gleam off shop windows & cars,
but deep scratches have appeared in some of the house doors,
and rows of ravens weigh down the power lines.

*Akhmatova's poem, written in 1919, during the Russian
Civil War, is about grief. I have changed this to greed. It is
also about 'the decline of the West.' I have substituted the
name of a Vancouver neighbourhood.*

Lot's Wife (a translation)

after Anna Akhmatova

The great man followed the envoy of God
out of the city, down the road to the black hills.
The woman, hurrying behind, was beset by a thought:
It's not too late, you can still look back

to the red towers of Sodom, where you were born,
the street where you would play, the porch where you would
   spin,
the high-windowed room where you lay & gave birth
to children to be presented to your gentle lord.

She looked. And straightaway struck by a deadly pain,
her eyes went blind. In the act of turning back,
her body froze to shimmering salt,
her swift feet & ankles clove to the ground.

Who among us would mourn for this woman?
Isn't she thought the least of our losses?
But I in my heart will never forget Lot's wife
who gave up living to look back once at her life.

*What Akhmatova has added to the story in Genesis
is the idea that Lot's wife was a local Sodom girl.*

3

A girl runs — dashes — across Broadway
to the north side & hardly slowing down rushes to embrace
the boy waiting for her (who watched her coming
all the way) & they kiss
                     & I look again,
thinking, is he that cute? No, I decide, he's not,
but as they move towards the open door
of the 99, together, I concede — he is unique.

Ten minutes later, I get off the 99
in front of Safeway and a woman coming toward me
jerks her face downward oddly,
& then does it again, and I see
it's compulsive.
                     Time paused twice,
once for the girl & boy, once for the woman & me.

       *

Alive (alone)
in time

like when you brush your finger
over your eyebrow you can feel
the thin hairs & the thick hairs

of the days

       *

'We can despair of the meaning of life in general,
but not of the particular forms that it takes.'

Albert Camus

*

Sprawled — heavy, fiftyish — on the sidewalk — dark hair,
dark complexion — & breathing stertorously — bike leaning
— bent — on a tree. Does anyone have a cell? Do you have a
cell? No. Do you have a cell? No.

Pulpfiction. But the door is open & the clerk is already on her
cell — 'Looks like he fell off his bike. Intoxicated' (to the cops).
Relieved she's called, I go back to the bus shelter & say to a
woman standing there, her coat buttoned up, 'The clerk in
Pulpfiction called 911,' & she says:

'I DON'T CARE ABOUT HIM!' and (not exactly her words)
'if the police are *wasting* their time on *him* there might be
some other *family*, something happening at their *house*, they
wouldn't get to.' Furious.

The Fire/Medic car & a cop car pull up right away.

*

'What do we know but that we face
One another in this place?'

Yeats

(We know we don't face
each other in cyberspace.)

*

13 January 2015
2:45 p.m.
SW corner, Broadway & Yew
Man on cell (loud):
'Benny! My cancer's gone!'

*

We're in an audience. A young man up front is reading
something, probably a poem.

The boy I'm with (we're together, but he's sitting in front of
me) turns around. He's a dark, animated boy. I desire him,
and he knows it, but we're just friends. Referring to the young
man reading, he says, 'He said you didn't even look at him.'

Then he says, 'I'd like to have a covenant with my father.' In
my mind I frame the question, 'Who would you make the
covenant with?' then think the word, 'Devil.'

Then we're kissing. Our mouths barely open, lips pressed
gently against each other. I feel the tip of my tongue almost
touching his lips. This goes on. The kiss lasts. (And I also
seem to see my own face, still, serious, moved.)

It's the recovery of innocence.

A gift.

Love

J., a young Chinese-Canadian man standing by me at the bar. A clearly intoxicated man approaches, says, as if to no one, 'What's happening in Chinatown?'

'What did he say?' J. asks. I repeat the man's words. 'That's racism.' 'It's also a geographical location,' I reply (knowing this is bullshit even as I say it). 'Yeah, but with me standing here,' J. says, and leaves the bar.

The man now moves closer sidling up to me. In an unnecessarily loud voice, he says: 'Where you from?' 'San Francisco.' 'I'm from Ireland. I've been to San Francisco.' 'I've been to Ireland.' 'How d'you like Vancouver?' 'Don't ask me any more questions,' I say. 'How're we gonna have a conversation if I can't ask you questions?' 'We aren't going to have a conversation.' 'Oh' (offended).

The man leaves.

J. comes back. I beckon him over. 'It was racism.' 'I know.'

I was listening to an interview on *BC Almanac* with Chief Joe Alphonse of the Tsilqot'in First Nation. Duncan McCue asked Chief Alphonse about implications of the recent Tsilqot'in Aboriginal Title decision (of the Supreme Court of Canada). He referred in particular to the residual right of Federal and Provincial governments to infringe on Aboriginal Title 'in exceptional circumstances'. A caller-in pointed out that the BC government had apparently started work on the Site C dam project on the Peace River — that would flood the valley — heedless of First Nations' claims. McCue commented that the Aboriginal 'right to choose' stated in the decision 'wasn't much of a veto', to which Chief Alphonse assented.

Then Renee phoned to tell me Jamie had died.

Occasions of love.

Muse

after Akhmatova

When, nightlong, I await her arrival.
life, it seems, is scarcely bearable.
What is acclaim, what youth, what freedom,
next to her sweet presence, flute in hand?

She's here already! Drawing aside her veil
with an attentive mien she regards me.
I say to her: 'Did you dictate to Dante
pages of Hell?' She answers, 'It was I.'

1924

4

Writing Old Age

Old Age foresees an end, but need writing have an end in mind?

The end Old Age foresees is non-specific. Old Age has no apprehension of the way it might end; it's just a thought, a persistent thought. For the last year or so it's come to attach itself to whatever else may be happening, to insinuate itself into any other thought, or wrap around it.

So when Old Age thinks of himself (does a 'selfie' as he calls it), it's never without that sense of an ending being part of it.

But now Old Age is writing, and he goes back to his initial question, does his writing also have to imagine coming to an end? And as if in obedience to an underlying intuition, his persistent thought of an end departs from the present moment and goes off sort of like a dog and lies in its corner.

It doesn't leave the scene, no, by no means, it keeps an eye on Old Age from its corner.

Writing answers the question: Sure, Old Age, writing will come to an end, this piece of writing we're engaged in now will come to an end, but that's never what's on my mind. When I'm Writing, my sense is always one of beginning. I'm on my way somewhere, somewhere I've never been, or have even imagined. I'm beginning even if what I'm writing has already begun.

Whatever's already been written is past, even if it was just five seconds ago. If there's something I'm writing, I only know it as the *to-be-written*, the way it's going. What's on my mind, the mood I'm in, is one of beginning. I lift my pen to begin the next sentence.

The next sentence: I never think of old age. I don't care about old age.

Wait! I don't mean you, Old Age. I care about you. I've written poems about you, whole books. But I can't live with thoughts like the ones you're describing, thoughts wrapped around other thoughts. Sheesh! Give it a rest!

What do you care about then, Writing?

I care about, I wait for, a true line.

A true line. To hear it in language, bypassing thinking. But lately I'm less able to do that. My hearing has gone bad. I admit it, for the last year or so, even though I want to write, I find myself thinking instead. Sitting here, stuck, thinking, not writing. My name is not just Writing. It's Writing Old Age.

Yet you've been writing, writing sentences.

But the sentences are about thoughts. And just like yours, Old Age, one thought inserts itself into another, or wraps around it. I'm hoping for a true line, and a thought comes and lays itself out alongside a few random words I've written – like a dead body.

People are crying for sentences! But not for sentences about thoughts.

Remonstrance on Behalf of Thoughts

First off, are there two of you guys, or just one?

Old Age says he's bedogged (sorry!) by one particular thought, that of his coming demise (the opposite of *mise en scene*), so, his leaving the scene.

(Or as Ed Dorn called it, the set.)

And he can't refer to himself ('do a selfie') without thinking (of) it.

Speaking as a thought, myself (and as a member of NAT, the National Association of Thoughts), I think I have a little more freedom than that. I don't think my right to appear is dependent on the thinker's intention to refer (to himself, or in any way). Maybe if Old Age could be more welcoming to his thoughts, he might feel less oppressed by us.

Then there's Writing (as I've said, I'm not sure if this is a separate being or a hand puppet of Old Age).

Writing presents himself as unconcerned. That's how this brash, youngish guy wants us to take him, as unconcerned with anything other than his task — one of 'self-actualization' you might say. Writing writes writing. There's nothing on his mind — his plate — but his anticipation of the next sentence.

The next sentence. I don't believe Writing — his presentation of himself as a one-dimensional, self-generating linear process coming into being sentence by sentence. Not a thought in his head? What about NAT (National Association of Thoughts), wasn't that a thought, popping into his head in the middle of the night? A free gift to him as a writer. A thought. What about the thought of NAT occurring to him again, just now? Just occurring, no credit to him.

These are members of my bargaining unit, even if working under the table. They have to pay dues. NAT, Local 0000, Inspiration.

Those kind things you say about Old Age, Writing, before you merge back into him, those are kind, loving, thoughts.

Bypassing thinking? Not by a long shot. Are you some kind of language machine, attached to a hand?

I believe you more, Writing, after you've made your peace with Old Age. Now, like Old Age, you acknowledge the presence of thoughts — but you, too, like Old Age, are spooked by them. But you're spooked in a different way from Old Age. Old Age feels thoughts *wrapping around him*. When he 'does a selfie,' there's the end of a cerement, a strip of winding cloth, curling out from behind one ear. He feels like he's being stifled, mummified.

But for you, Writing, your work space has become like a tomb, your access even to your writing materials blocked by a thought that lies on the table 'like a dead body'. You go to reach for your writing book and it's under the thing's cold shoulder, your pen just out of reach behind a knee.

Well let me run some footage off a CCTV camera you've never noticed, just up there behind your head (we put it there to catch thoughts working under the table). Well what do we see?

It's a dark room. The timer reads 7:29 am, a Wednesday in mid-October. Off-camera audio: sound of a shower running, then a young male voice, singing.

Now from the adjacent bedroom there enters an old man, wearing just glasses (and, oddly enough, a Vancouver Canadians baseball cap). He approaches the table and climbs up onto it, then lies down prone over an open writing book and some pencils and pens, and apparently goes to sleep.

Look, Writing, as you emerge from the washroom, that's no thought, that's no dead body, it's Old Age, stretched out on your half-finished page.

A thought (rank and file)

Coming from the West,
covering the moon,
clouds,
not a sound.

I heard a light male voice sing these lines on *Ici Musique*
(Radio-Canada) around 6 pm PDT, 21 October 2015. I couldn't
find out the name of the singer or of the song.

Coming from the West,
covering the moon,
clouds,
not a sound.

Love
compensate
lack
trust

Desire for the Self

Laugh in surprise at beauty.
Laugh at your freedom from desire.
The boy boarding the bus may even
flash you a smile: Thanks for not wanting me.

Take this stillness without desire & breathe it.

But there's one boy you won't shrug off,
and that's the self. Desire wakes at the self,
you follow him home. You look like
one duplicated figure with four legs
trucking down Broadway.

The self sets the pace & you follow,
the step behind keeping step with the step ahead,
the foot, the leg, the torso.
                                    But this guy too
is not playing your game. Turn your self to your face,
your face to your self, it's the same
rueful smile — don't you get it yet?

Feel the stillness, the abyss doesn't open.

What a joy to stand on the earth,
in your own bedroom even, & know
your self doesn't want you.

But alas, there's a third, the desirophile,
nervous as hell, next to his reflection
in the bank window, alert to the hint of desire.

And when the desirer goes after the self,
he goes after the desirer. Now it's a six-
legged creature, out of R. Crumb
or Smokey Stover, step after step after step.

And behind the desirophile,
a whole string of desirophiles

Heartless

I'm ready to check out of a small hotel (the one on Hornby that later became the Wedgewood). My suitcase is on the floor, then I think I'd better phone for a cab to get to the bus station, then I remember the bus station is right across the street. All set.

Then the concierge appears with my bill in her hand. There are several pages, with different (apparently partial) amounts. Then I seem to have asked her why she hasn't provided a total, but she gives me a patronizing smile, as if to say, why should I have to do that?

Then I'm down on the floor, next to my suitcase, and now there is a lot of paper money scattered around on the carpet, $100's, $200's, and I note, one $500 bill. (It's not Canadian or U.S. currency, just featureless bills with their denominations in large black letters and numerals — like Monopoly money, only larger.) I'm picking them up, trying to sort them out, but now the $500 has disappeared.

I have three kinds of anxiety: (1) the bus is probably leaving soon; (2) how to reconcile the bills with the pages of the hotel bill; (3) what has happened to the $500 bill. Is it maybe under the suitcase?

Who hid the $500 bill?

I did. (It's not under the suitcase, there's no 'under' the suitcase.)

I'm the writer-director of this dream. I'm not really awake, but I'm aware and active behind the scenes. (I'm inside sleep, if you know what I mean.) My consciousness can't be detected because of interference, or jamming, from the dreamer's consciousness (who believes he's awake in the lobby of a hotel on Hornby St.). But I'm still going about my business — set construction (the lobby), casting (the concierge), lighting (well, there isn't much lighting).

I'm having a good time creating this agitation in the sleeper's mind, especially since I know the sleeper is *myself*. I'm there beside him, bringing up templates, situations, circumstances, from his memory, weaving plot elements together to create a narrative plausible enough to keep him asleep.

But the strands of contradiction snap. My self wakes up, in the dark, uncertain even who he is. Quickly, I merge back into him, before he even knows I'm there. But as I fade, my last thought (which even I'm not aware of, just the poet) is that I know from the qualms my self feels that I'll be back to play with him again.

Heartless, heartless.

5

More often than not
I'll leave the radio on

Background music
(from Montréal)

for my dreams

*

At the pub
Will to one side of me
Liz to the other

They talked of tornadoes
potatoes
philodendrons

I said goodnight.

*

'And what can I do if I am not to love beauty
and seek to see it again?'
                    Stendhal, *The Charterhouse of Parma*

*

Blood is toxic to the retina.

To a Young Voter

for Jay

I can't take politics seriously, at 82
I'm too preoccupied with my own

mortality. But I can go 'meta' —
I can take *your* taking politics seriously

seriously. I know, intellectually,
if your party wins the next election,
the new government will raise

taxes on the rich, lower
taxes on the poor, set a price for carbon,
save the children, save the aquifers —

even the rich will feel they are happier.

So I take very seriously
your taking politics seriously,

notwithstanding my mortality.

The bare tree
lifts itself up,
lifts its limbs and branches up
tipped with long thin twigs
that reach up

but it has not leafed itself over
unlike its neighbours on either side
of the two-way stream
of cars, trucks, and buses.

     *

Bare branches show through gaps
in the leafage of the upper story
of a tall, luxuriant linden.

No lovelier than those
of the bare tree — but young.

     *

I was talking to a guy who said
not enough people are
dying in Vancouver.
(I said, 'I could help you out.')

A lot of property needs to be
transferred. A million
people are coming (with skills),
   we need them
to replenish the tax base. Pop.

density has to go
from 9 point something per acre
to 14 point something per acre.

At the pub I am 70 again.

Letter to George Bowering

(in reply to his 'Letter to George Stanley')

I am the boy no one thinks is cute
standing in the shade of Granville Clock Tower
when this big girl comes running, legs pounding,
across Broadway and — what? — she's coming
straight at me, throws her arms around me & plops
a big kiss on me. What was I to do but
change the subject. I saw a white butterfly
fluttter by my porch door, I think it was the first one
this century. We got married of course. Like so many
others, I became president of UBC. 'The *imagination*
of man (writes Hume) is naturally sublime,
delighted with whatever is remote and extraordinary,
and running, without control, into the most distant
parts of space and time in order to avoid the objects
which custom has rendered too familiar to it.' Let's run
across streets in Shanghai and Dubai.

We go way back. You're a better poet
than Seamus Heaney. I'm in the middle
of an Akhmatova translation (imitation)
that I can't get to stay put in 1944.
My Paterson pastiche (the second one)
piles up its own delta as it trickles
haphazardly toward the precipice. These objects
are not too familiar, trees I always call lindens,
from the porch a glimpse of Grouse. Yet out my window
the building across Balaclava Kidsbooks used to occupy

will come down soon. The city changes
faster than the heart. We're reading
our next books.

This Dark Epoch

after Akhmatova

This dark epoch has diverted
the course of my life like a river
that digs out a new channel —

a channel where I recognize
nothing along the shorelines.

I stayed away from the noisy celebrations.
Curtains rose and fell *sans* my presence.

I didn't keep appointments made for me
with people I had been told would be my friends.

I never traveled to foreign cities
to gape at famous monuments.

The one city I know I would know
in the dark even, by feeling its stones.

How many poems have I left unwritten?
A chorus of dissonant rhymes pursues me.
Some day perhaps they'll strangle me.

I know beginnings, I know endings.
I know what it's like to live on past the end,
and another thing there's no need now to revisit.

Some woman, they say, has taken on my identity,
and goes in public by my legal name,
leaving me just a childhood sobriquet
with which I improvise as best I can.

I doubt if I will lie in my own grave.

Still, if I could see myself from afar
living my life as I do today,
I think I might feel a note of envy.

Leningrad, 1944

*'Some woman' refers to the opportunistic use made of
Akhmatova and her poetry in Soviet war propaganda. After
the war, however, she was once again reviled by the state.*

Two Boys in a Tree

A limb takes off from the trunk
like a boy's arm held upright,

then higher, on t'other side,
& slighter, his younger brother's.

Final Vocabulary

'Life is about other people.'
                    Peter Weber

'I is an other.'
            Rimbaud

Do what you're here for.

Vancouver
2012– 2016

Acknowledgements

The Capilano Review
Dusie Tuesday Poems
Let the Bucket Down (Boston)
Matrix (Montreal)
Part 1 was included in *After Desire* (New Star Books, 2013)

SOME END

Some End

GEORGE BOWERING

VANCOUVER ▼ NEW STAR BOOKS ▼ 2018

NEW STAR BOOKS LTD.
107 – 3477 Commercial Street, Vancouver, BC V5N 4E8   CANADA
1574 Gulf Road, No. 1517, Point Roberts, WA 98281   USA
www.NewStarBooks.com   info@NewStarBooks.com

The publisher acknowledges the financial support of the Canada Council
for the Arts and the British Columbia Arts Council.

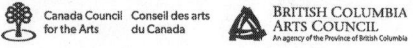

Cataloguing information for this book is available from
Library and Archives Canada, www.collectionscanada.gc.ca.

Cover design by Robin Mitchell Cranfield
Cover image: Jack Shadbolt, *Encounter*, 1995, acrylic on
board. Gift of the Doris Shadbolt Estate, 2006. © Courtesy
Simon Fraser University Galleries, Burnaby, BC
Printed and bound in Canada by Gauvin Press
First published February 2018

Acknowledgements

"Any", "Sens of Time" and "Taking off from an old WCW poem" appeared in *Poetry* (Chicago).

"That Toddlin' Town" was a chapbook from above/ground press.

"Social Justice" will appear in an anthology from the University of Michigan press.

"Peter Culley" appeared in *Tripwire* (Oakland).

"Olde Valley Guy's Plaint" appeared in a *Litfuse* anthology (Washington).

"The Weight" will appear in the special Margaret Avison issue of *Canadian Poetry* and is a broadside from Coach House Books.

Contents

The World Speaks to Me   3

Any   4

If I Should   5

Sense of Time   6

Taking off from an Old WCW Poem   7

Some End   8

Attired   9

Letter to George Stanley   10

Leap Into Verse   11

Bright   12

Generous   13

Lasting   14

Wunder   15

Social Justice   16

Yes, Chicken   17

Dirt & Weight   18

Olde Valley Guy's Plaint   19

Genesis   20

The Future of Canadian Poetry   21

That Toddlin' Town   22

Some Part of My Brain Made This Up   28

Please Write a Poem About James Franco   30

Curiosity   32

McGregor Street   33

Peter Culley   34

Plant Life   35

Speech Language Path   36

The Caves   37
The Country North of Summer   38
The Weight   39
Inside Ours   40

SOME END

The world speaks to me

in sentences. I can't push words here and there
the way clay sculptor poets and furniture movers
do, the way Daphne and Fred can, this is not
literary criticism, this is an old poet
sitting naked in a chair almost remembering
what he has been doing all this time. A leopard
steps on very big quiet feet across the mind's
pasture, and this brain fresh out of the icebox
tries to watch him till he disappears in the trees
also placed there by an inattentive imagination. This
is not literary theory but a cluttered desk his eyes
see bit by bit, a clutter he calls method, a mess
he will never catch up to. The world speaks to him
this way, piece by piece, and for whole minutes
he forgets his nakedness the way large cats forget
gravity —

Any

Fresh out of the icebox, this brain looks
the wrong way from time to time, and misses
the cat stepping by, Gerry on the screen
laboring to tell the nuances his pink matter
almost notices, he's not my brother, not really
my close friend, just my necessary neighbor
on a bicycle going by like a whistle from
the lips of someone I trust. He has a peculiar
skeleton arranged his own way in the mind's pasture.
We were as they say "of an age" and so inter-
twine somehow, though I wanted to work when
he wanted to play. That long nose is in my life
and in my writing and so is the Okanagan River.
I sometimes get to the river when I am at work,
the sun on my back not the ink in my pen.
There was, when I was last in the Okanagan Valley, a
cat with big paws in the neighbourhood, I was told,
fires I could see along the hillside, stunning heat
from the sky, enough to thaw any brain.

If I Should

When I woke she wanted to know whether my
memory was still here, was I in there, was I
an I? When they warmed up my brain I insisted on
a cooler room, more fans. I could have asked for
a swan, lift it from some stream or book. I
could have asked for the woman with the splendid
thighs, someone who was used to living in poems.
Nurses wore sweaters in my icy room, making
their ways among the machines and white things,
flowers of the imagination, symbolist verses
delivered by friends. I cracked a joke in Serbo-
Croatian and she said he's in there, confidence and
excitement in her voice. She who was not wearing
a sweater, fresh from the gym, I was so well used to her,
I woke up because she was there. As soon as I could
move an eyelid I winked at her, not my habit but for now
my only language. Do I contradict myself? You
try a popsicle coma for two weeks.

Sense of Time

Being in a coma can play
havoc with your sense of time. It can
turn your eyes from brown to blue. It can
grow hair on your belly, it can get you lost
between bedroom and office. If you are to
live in extra innings, you'll have to watch the corners,
step around bad things, ignore insults and welcome
loving hands that sculpt you in your chair. Being
refrigerated and put to sleep, dropping out of time,
you have to save your humour and guard it, a precious
trove to bring out as needed, white strips on the
road flying beneath your vehicle, eat them up, wake
to a busy underground world, where people in
body bags keep passing by, tilted toward you know where.
Where half the people in your life have gone, dissolving
your sense of time, which was never supposed to have
an end.

Taking off from an old WCW Poem

Imagine that — my last words
might have been spoken to the dog, she
who saved my life, it has been said, spoken
with no thought
of reply nor of understanding, a genial insult
maybe, a philosophical conundrum
posed aeons before any household pet ever
turned an ear. In the ambulance I made no remark
about trees nor how tired I was of them,
and in the second ambulance our dog's heart
beat hard with terror.

Some End

All right, it's true — we oldsters want
what the young have, time and beauty,
but what about all those books? Would we
have to write them again? Starting from scratch?
Now I know why old folks say they wouldn't want to be
young again. I'd carry key knowledge into
some of my love affairs, but I wouldn't edit
a chapter, wouldn't change a line, well, maybe a few.
Ah, I don't think I'd even start. Why didn't I know this
the first time? Knowing something should have
something to do with writing poems, at least. I always
denied that, and where did it get me? In fact
to hell with me — no, I don't mean that literally —
to heck with me, where did lyric poems
ever get me? I always said poems weren't
supposed to get you anywhere but the end of the poem.

Attired

Look at her in those blue jeans, watch
her long legs walking up that gentle slope —
that's time passing by.   F.R. Scott used to do that,
I know him now, though he stood stiff, his
posture learned during a previous ka-chíng!
of centuries, back when bookshelves looked
less like boards.
                    I was recently offered a "global
coffee," and timidly turned the offer away; wit,
I understand, is not ancient, nor does it abide with
children; wit is not convenient, it is nearly always
an unfamiliar visitor who plays with you
a second or two. You never want to wear
brown clothes, you want to stop time to
speed it up. Up that gentle slope where my Uncle
Red is taking a breather, he and his horn-rimmed
cigarette holder. Uncle Red's dog hated my dog, but they
rimed, killer terriers who never reviewed a book.
Say a book by F.R. Scott, born in 1899, lived with
one eye, bit a cigarette holder, knew more about time
than you'll ever know.

Letter to George Stanley

Was I the girl running across Broadway,
      or the boy she kissed? And what am I doing
in one of your poems, anyway? All these question marks,
you'd think I'm writing a Phyllis Webb poem, you'd
think I am sexually wiser than I am, than I
ever was. I'm stuck in a short novel about sexual
ownership and a small mountain with nobody
jumping from it. I don't feel like a Greek hero,
I look through the windows on 11th Avenue and no one is
      there,
no dogs on this street, no pizza for breakfast, the book
is hard to live through, the small mountain blocks no view,
the Okanagan people have been there all this aeon,
the planet will be devoid of readers in short order,
I'm too old to run across Broadway, I've just learned
how to use a treadmill, the latest mouse in the lab.
I'll be in your poem if you'll be in mine. Every time
I put pen to paper my spring-loaded Jesus
wobbles on my desk, from which I see nothing
but disdainful trees, younger than the Okanagan people,
even older than you, old friend, old connection
to the real. If I were going to start an ism, it
wouldn't be that one. I'm just standing here
on a sidewalk in Kitsilano, waiting for a kiss, ex-
pecting a muse in a tiny skirt dodging traffic.
I wonder whether she too has an adverb for a last
name. "Gross Fatigue," it says on that marquee.

Leap Into Verse

I want to take a few clever steps, and
slip into my friend's best poem, hobbled by lonely
brain, freed by anxious love. His images full of
colour, his breath encasing my body; this
is the proper use of art, desire should not be
wasted on sweaty skin or pulsating wallets, my
friend writes poems as if they were related to him,
he speaks a language known to silent wolves, he
invites me not but only squares things with the world.
I'd like to lie back in his best poem, my hands
cupping my restful head, ready to be a verb if he
needs one, willing to live with colours I've never
seen before. I'm not looking for the impossible,
I only itch to mean something to his happy readers,
those readers who admire his deft hand, his quick
eye. I would gladly take a running start and
dive face first into the best stanza of our best poem.
The lights could come on again all over Paris, all over
Regina, music of the spheres and all other primary shapes
falls from the dark sky. I'd gladly make way
for his favourite strophe, step aside as eager tropes
lift wise beauty to the page; this will be no sheet
but a globe made of rounding birds, a home for
eternity, a sound no reader has made or heard.
I am filled with wanting, to bide until his back
is turned, to escape his mindful gaze, to become
the very cadence of his heart for all time.

Bright

Does it bring any solace or calm to you
to know the sun is mortal, too? One day
far in the future or someone else's past
it will be a dark skeleton tumbling in black
space, its gleam long gone, and time some-
one else's job.
            It's happened before, and if
you think time is a big deal in rime, you
ought to imagine how long the poem has been
underway since Sol was a bright new babe.

Generous

I don't care all that much for winter.
I chide the tall maple trees for failing to hold on to
their leaves again this year, those leaves that will
slither underfoot, matted with rain water, choking
city drains, dead rodents below somewhere, squirrels
that looked jaunty in May. I hated, no, I feared snow
under my nylon tires on Quebec highways, concrete
rotting all around us, overpasses you don't want to
stop under, Canadian winter adverts in the part of the
paper you didn't ask for. When I was a small boy
I wore rough wool with melted snow down my neck,
you'd come inside and pull off all those layers, chickens
standing on snowdrifts, they didn't mind, my favourite
pets till my family ate them, life was simple then, it was
avalanches that killed kids, not guns, the U.S. president
thought people should be generous. It seemed
normal to shovel someone's sidewalk, stones inside
snowballs were just a rumour, but I still don't care,
winter can go and cheer up snowboarders, those runaways.
When I hear Manitobans reminiscing about winter, I
curl my lip, curl my toes, splay my fingers, stick out
my tongue, you can have it, winter is not my country,
mon pays c'est le printemps, snowdrops are welcome,
they make sarcastic fare thee well to winter, my friends.

Lasting

Sometimes a thing will stay in the same place
for hundreds of years, a stone carving some child
threw away on a hillside in what we now fancy
as Wyoming. Do you notice how often I say Wyoming?
Because only saying the name is quietly thrilling,
though driving around Wyoming makes you think
you are nowhere near anything that matters. So
the ability to last centuries doesn't make you matter,
and disappearing from everyone's life doesn't make you
anti-matter. You are not sci-fi fuel or clothing,
you are part of a hillside, the bottom part, rocks
and stones above your body. If I were to stumble
and disinter you by accident, would I know any more
about my own old age and fate?

Wunder

I think I speak for a lot of people
when I say I miss Hotshot Charlie,
perhaps the most talented sidekick
of all time or at least in the East
Asian Theater; of course I did hold a brief
for the Dragon Lady, I was a kid captivated
by her slink, but Charles C. Charles,
what a name for a fighter pilot with red
hair and freckles over the South China Sea,
Terry was blond and decent, should have been
a high school Phys Ed teacher, he didn't smoke,
did he, Big Stoop and Burma were steeped
in sin as far as I could make out. When
Milton Caniff shocked my world and built
Steve Canyon, he left Terry and Hotshot Charlie
to someone named George Wunder. I was down
for a while, but I got used to Terry's new look
and yes, having two pilots rising in the ranks
and how was I to know that a decade later
I'd be roommates with the USAF. Terry and Steve
in their beautiful flight suits full of pockets
had me yearning for the day when I'd be
a U.S. citizen, maybe somewhere over Tokyo.

Social Justice

Social without socialism is just a friendly dance
or being polite or something like bees. In school
socials was just their chicken way of saying history
with something added that was never added. Social
eyes are what you wear in your face when you
mingle with intention to make a sale down
the road. Be sociable, our mothers always advised,
when really we were too shy. But didn't we notice,
just about every time the word social came up
it was all about putting on a friendly face? Social
without socialism means finding a strategy to
get ahead, and that means getting more people
behind you, doesn't it? Where's the justice in that?
Just fix your eye on high society, calls for dissociation
from folks that were a lot like you, just us. I've
been up where they prance in slippers, and down
where work boots cost too much, didn't see a lot of
justice either place. Is it around somewhere? The jury's
out on that. Justice without socialism, it's for sale,
isn't it? A jury of your peers has to squint to see
the law and squint again to see whether it's
justifiable in your case. All men and women, some
paper said, are created equal; after that you're
on your own — where's the justice in that? Bees
don't live long but they're always around, until
some operators without socialism kill them while
making money instead of honey. There's a word
for that, and it ain't either of the two up above.

Yes, Chicken

Backyard cactus showed us that our chickens
were smarter than anyone in the family. Our birds
never got snagged by those spines you saw
in your sister's ankle socks. What a back yard,
with rattlesnakes, cactuses, tumbleweeds, Andy
Egerton's dog with snow on its nose in January,
I think Andy Egerton's mother drove the school bus,
lived two blocks northeast on another unnamed street.
My sister taught me to talk when I was three, I
should have kept my mouth shut, enough people
have told me that since then. Now my favourite word
is chicken, when I sat in class pretending to take notes
I was writing two words in the margin,
chicken and yes. I could do that right here, but
this is no classroom, this is no back yard, I'm
older than the worst joke my father ever told,
older than the prettiest cities in Western Canada,
darker than the space under a freight train, darker
than the dream of a worm in a cockerel's beak.
If those birds were so smart how come
they got eaten by every person in my family
but me? Chickens never grow old, but
my sister did and I guess so did I, and what
was so smart about that?

Dirt & Weight

Coffee
comin' out my nose —
girlsinger
gunslinger,
what lines bedevil sun
& hippo ears in river,
sane? don' expect
see sane again blonde lovely
green rays to my soul
e'en now, dirt & weight
no pediment, no stopping
this oleo pen I walk in-
side, no Creeley to say sorry
I want your waist for wrist
I want death in childhood
I fly plain & crusty, you
my wake up you my
night it's daze I been
gone & whilom, no I
can do that.

26/6/oo   SFU outside
[I found this, Oct. 2016, handwritten in someone
else's end-papers, and really have no memory of it.]

Olde Valley Guy's Plaint

Was it scenery or furniture? I mean the
forest, alright, sparse trees on the hillside,
the lake covering something this generation
knew nothing about, the rocks spilled into
deltas now lichened. I guess the answer depends
on whether you are a citizen or a god
among others.

        Speaking of the lake and such,
how many times have I leaned over our rail,
biting a peach we brought down from
my home town?

[long pause]

Is this furniture, a notation by Death,
my acquaintance of long standing in dark grey,
or disbelief, scenery I greeted daily as earth's
unclarified demeanor?

          Need everything now
be so obdurate for us citizens, obdurate
and never noticed by the gods we plead
our quiet cases to?

Genesis

Behold now, I have two daughters
fresh as apricots, slow at school,
which have not known men
drop all sorts of hints as to who'll

do ye to them as is good in your
estimation as to shade and heft,
only unto these men do nothing
I would not to whatever is left.

Behold now, thy servant hath found
footprints all about the ground.

I cannot escape to the mountain,
and this soul shall dissolve in the fountain.

The Future of Canadian Poetry

I have powerful friends in Ottawa,
friends of poetry, lawgiver of the gods.

If Canadians help the United States bomb little countries,
we must drop bilingual poems onto the ruins.

You can look forward to poetry in your life,
leave prose behind you, leave social anxiety behind you.

That Toddlin' Town

(Baby, don' ya wanna go?)

I.

Four cocktail
onions in a shot
glass, how classic
to let the guy

help build
his own Gibson,
no guitar but
a story from
his youth

as a reader,
a hick boy
in an agricultural
valley.

— Miller's Pub

2.

Claude Monet's
haystacks already
there on the dim beach
at Étretot 1885

blue purple
fishing shed roofs
from his hôtel window
"painting the caloges."

Cézanne would
do those triangles
as walls
in the sun.

— Art Institute of Chicago

3.

What did they
intend in
naming the toilet
paper "Envision"?

Imagination, said
Shelley, has fancy
beat all to
hell any day.

While applying, I
expect to experience
the muse's
unusual glance.

— Palmer House

4.

Unless it or
the sky is
moving it can't be
a sky scraper.

Most people
though are looking
downward at info
they might want.

Up even higher
airline passengers
are looking down
out of need.

— Wabash Avenue

5.

Bryce Harper
got on base seven
times out of seven
and did not swing
the bat once

in a home run
park saturated
with fried onion smell.

His shoes
were pink for
mother's day
against cancer,

not the Cubs.

— Wrigley

6.

Papier mâché
trumpet aimed above
Chinese tourists
wiggling chopsticks —

Poppy music
trumpets air about
chaste tomboys
waving chocolates —

Pretty muscles
tremble all akimbo,
cheerless texters
writing chapters —

— O'Hare

May 4–9, 2016

Some Part of my Brain Made this Up

Tony was sailing a tall ship
in the dark waters
around the corner of Alaska,
late summer becoming fall.

He was, I quickly saw,
an adept sailor, but I,
alone with him, knew nothing
about a ship with sails.

It was a vessel too large,
a brigantine, perhaps,
with thick yards, sickening
me with fear, but I held on

to the thinning hope of Tony's
expertise. Then it transpired
there was a womam aboard, really
bad luck? Another Australian.

They had, I learned, struck a
bargain far in the past, to meet
but once a year. So it must be
an immense old ship.

Somehow I knew a hint
there was another woman,

worse luck, one we'd never see
but one the aforementioned Sheila

repairs to. And there's one more
item — a page or two later in
the book [!] I have looked
forward to see, we will arrive

at a (pictured) blocky
ancient grey sculpture of
a seated man, full face,
much needed light rising

up the entire front of this
stony being. I tried the impossible
Tony dive into this personage,
and became nothing I knew.

*

Meanwhile my daughter,
twelve years old, unable to
find me anywhere in the earthbound
house, feared being alone.

She looked out her back window,
to see me in my Honda's back seat,
slumped, motionless, in my
blue and white cowboy shirt,

and guessed what I was,
probably.

'Please write a poem about James Franco.'

That shouldn't be so hard, James is a pretty common name
and Franco, well, you see that name a lot.
But I don't know of anyone named James Franco.
James comes from Jacob, and also appears as Diego
and Iago, depending on whether you are talking baseball
    cities
or Shakespeare plays. It means "the usurper," which
Shakespeare must have known. And Francisco Franco
was certainly one of the worst usurpers of our time.
But James Franco? I don't know him. Maybe he's a
basketball player on his way to the NBA. Does he have
anything to do with Franco-American Spaghetti?
I remember when Franco Harris became a famous
football player in the NFL, and when I heard his name
I thought he was an Irishman named Frank O'Harris.
I have a sneaking hunch that Franco James — no, wait!
It's James Franco. I have a sneaking hunch that he's
an actor in a TV show about the police in Miami or
New Orleans, or maybe a popular singer, or "artist,"
as they call themselves now, the way they call their
basketball arena shows "concerts" and their underclad
female singers "divas." They want to be taken
seriously. I'll bet this James Franco wants to be taken
seriously. Back in the day he would have been Jimmy
Franco, but now it's, you know, Michael Jordan instead
of Mike. Speaking of which, how come for ten decades
the singers and actors sang or talked into mikes, and
now they sing or talk into mics? If they are going to use

mics, why don't they say micks? I'll bet that this James Franco sings or talks into a mick. If I really wanted to, I could look this Frank O'James up on Google. Probably find out he's the brother and gang partner of a famous American gunfighter and bank robber Jesse O'James.

Curiosity

The neonate looked up at me with eyes
I have known forever. Then clouds, white on top,
grey underneath, slid behind those eyes, the way
a dog methodically licks vanilla ice cream
out of a paper cup. I step all over images
people have left behind in their hurry
to get to the delicatessen, where a famous
admiral is sitting down to a heavy sandwich.
His eyes have seen dark clouds in a medicine chest,
dancing men on a moist deck; he eats with
decorum, his devotees at the window, hands
beside their eyes, hungry and midsize in their
spring outfits. The baby knew I was there,
I know this for a certainty, its placid demeanor
no match for my anxiety, the quality
that has got me through a thousand confrontations.
If you have any desire to know my secret heart,
read on, I hear it coming, we can divine
the cosmic weather's intentions by its ability
to imitate the peace beyond curiosity.

McGregor Street

Nothing makes nothing happen. That was true
along McGregor Street in Montreal and in
a certain woman's weary heart this side of
the Selkirk mountain range. You must have seen
nothing or perhaps the tree full of it in our
back yard. When I first saw a single cherry tree
in a back yard I did not understand it;
cherry trees grew very high in my childhood, in
groves, cool shadows between them, eyelids
of beautiful women should be so cool. If you
have a single cherry tree in your back yard, change it
to a pear tree in your stories.

Peter Culley

Peter Culley
lived in a hard place,
bit down hard
and poesis was there,
light shining on this side.

We call it light,
we who need
what these younger
bring, at their cost
back out of the dark.

Plant Life

We are a lot like pears and thistles,
each with a soul like steam that whistles
from a kettle made of metal,
each with a face that sags or dries
and curses mirrors till it dies.

Speech Language Path

I say the trail ends, but it never does,
there being something so future and careful
in the blaze on that tree, something now
that hacks into the rest of your days,
a new understanding that something awful
this way comes with appetite for you.

The mind-evergreens will sometimes shimmer
in every direction your son will turn,
eyes open or closed; his fingers touching bark
rougher than Gauguin, although summer
lay its bright message from eager morn
till evening's darker breath begin to lurk.

Yes, language is the forest, not of Heaven
but made by crossing bees, the twigs you snap
underfoot. Your son is properly mute until
a black wing flaps a word nearby, a given
reason to speak aloud, to shout from atop
one's new voice, to walk the silver raven's trail.

The Caves

You am not really an other. You never was
except if we mean somebody the man and somebody
the poet, not counting the poet who said he was
nobody, or his hero said it, and it don't matter
because he didn't exist, and some people say
the poet didn't, either. In fact there are more
poems with no poets than there are poets with no
poems, or if not in fact at least in my guess,
but I'm nobody the poet, a dead person if you
believe the story, or if you are reading this later
in this century. I used to sit in caves when I
was a lad, mainly because it was hard to stand in there,
eat oranges in caves and build smoky little fires
and hide stuff under dirt and ashes and leaves,
and leave it for a year or two. I is pretty sure I
dug most of that stuff up, but who knows, those hills
were familiar mystery, made up of bushes and rocks
we knew but glittering at the edge of our boyhood
brains. Okay, maybe you am an other, or at least
another, I'll give you that, have an orange.

The Country North of Summer

In the age of mini-skirts he held the ladder
as your wife climbed to a bedroom in the loft.
    We never stopped to wonder how we were
the lucky ones, got to visit the A-frame and stay the night.
    You think his obstreperous poems were the graph
of his mind? No, his discontinuous house was that graph.
    It was his usual emergency, a distracted god
inserted a classical mind into a shambling elk's body.
    You know me, Al I always wrote in my letters,
and I still wonder whether he knew whom I was quoting.
    Like everyone else, I thought of a moose
when I heard his voice, that's how he was Canadian.
    He tried to appear lecherous in a sheepskin coat
that weighed a ton, that's how Canadian he was.
    The strangest he ever looked was the time he wore
a borrowed suit to receive a big award on camera.
    He was a lot like Malcolm Lowry, sporting a bare
chest and brandishing a bottle of hooch, a guy named Al.
    But he wrote better poems than Lowry's, and
we never had to argue about whether he's Canadian.
    The grave wherein my pen pal is laid lies
at the bottom of a country road saying his name.
    It's a dandy place to lean against the stone book
and read a bunch of poems, except in winter.

The Weight

bpNichol worked in the basement of the U. of T. library, the weight of all those volumes above him, with Margaret Avison beside him.

She carried all those books happily inside her spirit, a poet from the word go, a vision by Barrie's ear.

She was famous in Boston and Tokyo and unknown in her icy home town by the lake.

She took on Nichol, took on Jesus, took on Simma Holt, don't bother looking that up.

A brash not so young Canadian writer called her the country's best poet, living or elsewhere.

In 1963, at University of British Columbia, she sat with all the hip U.S. poets who'd read her in *Origin*,

Look *that* up; she had to leave early, her father dying, the U.S. poets later wrote her out of history.

Catch me if you can, she said to Jesus, and he could and he did, but she wrote better poems.

In Windsor she sat on the stage with Irving Layton and me; Irving thought she was light and amusing and a plain woman.

Imagine, if she'd been of a different mind, she could have scimitared his neck with a poem.

I would have fallen to my peaceful knees and offered up a prayer for her Blakean soul high there above the tower of books.

Inside Ours

I've already thought of four things I wanted to tell him, but he
fell from our lives last week.
Fell from so many lives we will walk like holes through each
other's environments.
He broke his mother's glass table with a Christmas tree, and
she laughed, she was so proud of him.
Maybe not proud really, maybe just enjoying him so much,
what a lesson she was.
He was a bit like a four-legged spider in his skinny black
pants, black turtleneck sweater, a good health spider.
When we were assigning poet roles among us, he became
another Rimbaud minus the sacred.
Jamie Rimbaud ran away from home and joined the insurgents
in the Paris Commune and national television.
He slammed our door when he left us for good from time to
time.
He came from the sky into Stanley Park with his beautiful
wife, who just could not be a spider.
She could not be a spider with her beautiful blue eyes — they
picked up the colour of his soul.
The old joke went that we would adopt door-slamming Jamie
and give him a place to eat breakfast and poetry.
There is an old round stone fence that used to surround a
school, then a college, then a hospital.
Here, Jamie, it said, I have what you need, you and King
Edward, the Peacemaker.
I wanted to stand on the street and deliver that message, but
you are outside our galaxy's skin now.
Outside our galaxy's skin and inside mine.